The King On Trial

Storyline **Verlie Ward**
Illustrations **Steven Butler**

Pilate, the Roman governor, was sleeping peacefully. Suddenly there was a knock at his door. His servant entered and told Pilate a prisoner had been sentenced to death. As governer, Pilate had to sign the papers.

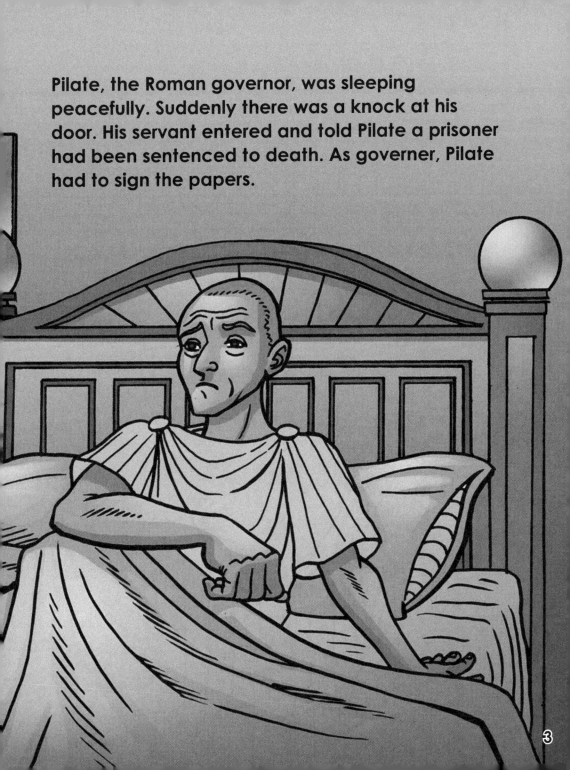

As he walked into the judgment hall, Pilate was tired and grumpy. But when he looked into the face of the prisoner, he was surprised. This man did not look like a criminal. Pilate could see goodness, kindness, and love in his face. Pilate's servant told him the man was Jesus.

Pilate had heard about Jesus. He had heard about the miracles of healing. He wanted to find out more. Pilate did not want to condemn an innocent man. He waited to hear the charges the Jews brought against Jesus.

The priests had hired a man to tell lies. This man said, "Jesus is a very bad man. He does not pay taxes to Caesar. He even declares himself to be king."

But Pilate did not believe the man. Pilate did not believe that Jesus was bad.

So Pilate turned to Jesus. "Are you the King of the Jews?" he asked.

Jesus quietly replied, "It is as you say." As Jesus spoke, his face glowed. The whole room seemed full of light.

Pilate heard the noisy crowds shouting outside. He went to them and called out, "I find no fault in him."

But the people were angry at Pilate's judgment, and Pilate wanted the people to like him. When he heard that Jesus was from Galilee he thought to himself, "I will get rid of this problem. I will send the man to Herod."

Many priests and elders followed Jesus and the soldiers to Herod's judgment hall.

Herod had heard stories about Jesus. "I want to ask this man some questions," he said. But mostly Herod wanted to see Jesus perform some kind of miracle.

Herod asked many questions, but Jesus didn't speak. Finally Herod told Jesus that if he would perform just one simple miracle he could go free.

The crowd became very angry. They thought Jesus might be released. They began to shout angry words. But Jesus still did nothing.

Herod and his soldiers began to make fun of Jesus. They placed a royal robe around his shoulders. They bowed down mocking him.

But Jesus did not respond to their insults. Then Herod became afraid. He wanted nothing more to do with Jesus. So Herod sent Jesus back to Pilate.

Pilate was not happy when he saw Jesus again. "I have already judged this man and found him innocent," he told the people. "I will beat him and let him go." Pilate thought that this would satisfy the crowd.

Just then a servant arrived with a message from Pilate's wife. She'd had a frightening dream about Jesus. "Have nothing to do with this man," she wrote.

Pilate was very concerned. He trusted his wife, but he knew he must act at once. He was very troubled.

So Pilate called out to the crowd, "Shall I set this man free?" But the crowd shouted back, "Crucify him!"

"Why, what evil has he done?" Pilate asked. "I will beat him and let him go."

But the angry crowd shouted out again and again, "Crucify him!" "Crucify him!"

Suddenly Pilate remembered a custom that might save Jesus. It was a tradition to free one prisoner chosen by the people.

Pilate thought of Barabbas, a very evil man who had committed many crimes. So Pilate sent for Barabbas and stood him beside Jesus.

"Who shall I release?" asked Pilate. "Barabbas or Jesus?"

To Pilate's amazement, the people shouted "Barabbas!" "Then what shall I do with Jesus?" he asked.

"Crucify him!" the angry crowd shouted.

"Shall I crucify your king?" asked Pilate in surprise.

"We have no king but Caesar!" the people shouted.

Pilate saw he could not change the minds of the people. He called for a basin of water and washed his hands in front of them. "I am innocent of this man's blood!" he shouted. "The responsibility is yours!"

Then the high priest answered, "His blood be on us and our children!" And the crowd agreed, chanting the priest's angry words.

Then Pilate let Barabbas go free and handed Jesus over to the angry mob to be crucified.

And this was the beginning of the saddest day in all of earth's history.